D1506817

INSPIRATIONAL QUOTES

365 BEST INSPIRATIONAL QUOTES FOR DAILY
MOTIVATION

Paul Brown

More Books By Paul Brown

The 1000 Best Quotes Of All Time

ISBN: 9798706161194

INTRODUCTION

Sometimes, we need to keep some inspirational quotes or speeches to inspire us when we're down. And what better way than keep them all in one place? That way we don't have to look for them. The best way is via a book, which is why I created this book of 365 inspirational quotes for every day of the year.

Each day, a new quote will be waiting for you. The quotes are small gems, unique in their own right, that will slowly transform your behavior and add a new source of motivation to your life. Each quote was carefully selected because of its inspirational value and ability to change the way you view your life. Just a few good quotes a day could inspire you to do great things, whether it's about starting a business, fulfilling the dreams you have for yourself, or even just bettering yourself on a daily basis.

Without further ado, here are some of the most inspiring, powerful and famous quotes I have collected over the years. Each and everyday I read two quotes. It's a great way to start your day! I hope you'll love them.

#1

"Somebody should tell us, right at the start of our lives, that we are dying. Then we might live life to the limit, every minute of every day. Do it! I say. Whatever you want to do, do it now! There are only so many tomorrows."

— **Michael Landon**

#2

"I am an old man and have known a great many troubles, but most of them never happened."

— **Mark Twain**

#3

"Start by doing what is necessary, then what is possible, and suddenly you are doing the impossible."

— **Francis of Assisi**

#4

"If opportunity doesn't knock, build a door"

— **Milton Berle**

#5

"You have brains in your head. You have feet in your shoes. You can steer yourself any direction you choose. You're on your own. And you know what you know. And YOU are the one who'll decide where to go..."

— Dr. Seuss

#6

"Be yourself; everyone else is already taken."

— Oscar Wilde

#7

"Be the change that you wish to see in the world."

— Mahatma Gandhi

#8

"Twenty years from now, you will be more disappointed by the things that you didn't do than by the ones you did do, so throw off the bowlines, sail away from safe harbor, catch the trade winds in your sails. Explore, Dream, Discover."

— Mark Twain

#9

"The best and most beautiful things in the world cannot be seen or even touched. They must be felt with the heart"

— Helen Keller

#10

"Yesterday is history, tomorrow is a mystery, today is a gift of God, which is why we call it the present."

— **Bil Keane**

#11

"I have not failed. I've just found 10,000 ways that won't work."

— **Thomas A. Edison**

#12

"Life isn't about finding yourself. Life is about creating yourself."

— **George Bernard Shaw**

#13

"There is no greater agony than bearing an untold story inside you."

— **Maya Angelou**

#14

"No one can make you feel inferior without your consent."

— **Eleanor Roosevelt**

#15

Whenever you find yourself on the side of the majority, it is time to pause and reflect.

— **Mark Twain**

#16

"Put your heart, mind, intellect, and soul even to your smallest acts. This is the secret of success"

— Sivananda Saraswati

#17

"Do what you can, with what you have, where you are."

— Theodore Roosevelt

#18

What great thing would you attempt if you knew you could not fail?

— Robert H. Schuller

#19

"Success is not final, failure is not fatal: it is the courage to continue that counts."

— Winston S. Churchill

#20

"Perfection is not attainable, but if we chase perfection we can catch excellence."

—Vince Lombardi

#21

"Your time is limited, so don't waste it living someone else's life."

— Steve Jobs

#22

"What you're supposed to do when you don't like a thing is change it. If you can't change it, change the way you think about it. Don't complain."

— Maya Angelou

#23

"First they ignore you, then they ridicule you, then they fight you, and then you win."

— Mahatma Gandhi

#24

"When everything seems to be going against you, remember that the airplane takes off against the wind, not with it."

— Henry Ford

#25

"Whatever you are, be a good one."

— Abraham Lincoln

#26

"Peace begins with a smile."

— Mother Teresa

#27

I've missed more than 9000 shots in my career. I've lost almost 300 games. 26 times, I've been trusted to take the game winning shot and missed. I've failed over and over and over again in my life. And that is why I succeed.

— Michael Jordan

#28

"Follow your bliss and the universe will open doors for you where there were only walls."

— Joseph Campbell

#29

"Live as if you were to die tomorrow. Learn as if you were to live forever."

— Mahatma Gandhi

#30

"Two wrongs don't make a right, but they make a good excuse."

— Thomas Stephen Szasz

#31

"What lies behind us and what lies before us are tiny matters compared to what lies within us."

— Ralph Waldo Emerson

#32

"When one door of happiness closes, another opens; but often we look so long at the closed door that we do not see the one which has been opened for us."

— Helen Keller

#33

"When I despair, I remember that all through history the way of truth and love have always won. There have been tyrants and murderers, and for a time, they can seem invincible, but in the end, they always fall. Think of it——always."

— Mahatma Gandhi

#34

"Nothing is impossible, the word itself says 'I'm possible'!"

— Audrey Hepburn

#35

"There are only two ways to live your life. One is as though nothing is a miracle. The other is as though everything is a miracle."

— Albert Einstein

#36

"Remembering that you are going to die is the best way I know to avoid the trap of thinking you have something to lose. You are already naked. There is no reason not to follow your heart."

— Steve Jobs

#37

"Welcome to today. Another day. Another chance. Feel free to change."

— Unknown

#38

"Do one thing every day that scares you."

— Eleanor Roosevelt

#39

"Never doubt that a small group of thoughtful, committed, citizens can change the world. Indeed, it is the only thing that ever has."

— Margaret Mead

#40

"I am not what happened to me, I am what I choose to become."

— C.G. Jung

#41

"You are the average of the five people you spend the most time with."

— Jim Rohn

#42

"Happiness is not something ready made. It comes from your own actions."

— Dalai Lama

#43

"What we fear doing most is usually what we most need to do."

— Timothy Ferriss

#44

"I am enough of an artist to draw freely upon my imagination. Imagination is more important than knowledge. Knowledge is limited. Imagination encircles the world."

— Albert Einstein

#45

"Live life fully while you're here. Experience everything. Take care of yourself and your friends. Have fun, be crazy, be weird. Go out and screw up! You're going to anyway, so you might as well enjoy the process. Take the opportunity to learn from your mistakes: find the cause of your problem and eliminate it. Don't try to be perfect; just be an excellent example of being human."

— Anthony Robbins

#46

You miss 100% of the shots you don't take.

—Wayne Gretzky

#47

"I can't change the direction of the wind, but I can adjust my sails to always reach my destination."

— Jimmy Dean

#48

Strive not to be a success, but rather to be of value.

–Albert Einstein

#49

"Always do what you are afraid to do."

— Ralph Waldo Emerson

#50

"Our lives begin to end the day we become silent about things that matter."

— Martin Luther King Jr.

#51

"When I was 5 years old, my mother always told me that happiness was the key to life. When I went to school, they asked me what I wanted to be when I grew up. I wrote down 'happy'. They told me I didn't understand the assignment, and I told them they didn't understand life."

— John Lennon

#52

"Talent hits a target no one else can hit. Genius hits a target no one else can see."

— Arthur Schopenhauer

#53

"Waiting is painful. Forgetting is painful. But not knowing which to do is the worst kind of suffering."

— Paulo Coelho

#54

"You might well remember that nothing can bring you success but yourself."

— Napoleon Hill

#55

Whatever the mind of man can conceive and believe, it can achieve.

–Napoleon Hill

#56

"May you live every day of your life."

— Jonathan Swift

#57

"Do not let your fire go out, spark by irreplaceable spark in the hopeless swamps of the not—quite, the not—yet, and the not—at—all. Do not let the hero in your soul perish in lonely frustration for the life you deserved and have never been able to reach. The world you desire can be won. It exists.. it is real.. it is possible.. it's yours."

— Ayn Rand

#58

"In the end, we will remember not the words of our enemies, but the silence of our friends."

— Martin Luther King Jr.

#59

"If you can't you must, and if you must you can."

— Anthony Robbins

#60

"Don't wish it were easier. Wish you were better."

— Jim Rohn

#61

"It isn't what you have or who you are or where you are or what you are doing that makes you happy or unhappy. It is what you think about it."

— **Dale Carnegie**

#62

"None but ourselves can free our minds."

— **Bob Marley**

#63

"Pain is temporary. Quitting lasts forever."

— **Lance Armstrong**

#64

"You never fail until you stop trying."

— **Albert Einstein**

#65

"Well, now

If little by little you stop loving me

I shall stop loving you

Little by little

If suddenly you forget me

Do not look for me

For I shall already have forgotten you

If you think it long and mad the wind of banners that passes through my life

And you decide to leave me at the shore of the heart where I have roots

Remember

That on that day, at that hour, I shall lift my arms

And my roots will set off to seek another land"

— Pablo Neruda

#66

"Prayer is not asking. It is a longing of the soul. It is daily admission of one's weakness. It is better in prayer to have a heart without words than words without a heart."

— Mahatma Gandhi

#67

"If she's amazing, she won't be easy. If she's easy, she won't be amazing. If she's worth it, you wont give up. If you give up, you're not worthy. ... Truth is, everybody is going to hurt you; you just gotta find the ones worth suffering for."

— Bob Marley

#68

"Hope is the thing with feathers

That perches in the soul

And sings the tune without the words

And never stops at all."

— Emily Dickinson

#69

"The future belongs to those who believe in the beauty of their dreams."

— Eleanor Roosevelt

#70

"It is so hard to leave—until you leave. And then it is the easiest goddamned thing in the world."

— John Green

#71

"There is neither happiness nor misery in the world; there is only the comparison of one state with another, nothing more. He who has felt the deepest grief is best able to experience supreme happiness. We must have felt what it is to die, Morrel, that we may appreciate the enjoyments of life. " Live, then, and be happy, beloved children of my heart, and never forget, that until the day God will deign to reveal the future to man, all human wisdom is contained in these two words, 'Wait and Hope."

— **Alexandre Dumas**

#72

The more you praise and celebrate your life, the more there is in life to celebrate.

— **Oprah Winfrey**

#73

"I like living. I have sometimes been wildly, despairingly, acutely miserable, racked with sorrow; but through it all I still know quite certainly that just to be alive is a grand thing."

— **Agatha Christie**

#74

"If there is no struggle, there is no progress."

—**Frederick Douglass**

#75

"The mind is its own place, and in itself can make a heaven of hell, a hell of heaven."

— **John Milton**

#76

"You is kind. You is smart. You is important."

— Kathryn Stockett

#77

"I've come to believe that all my past failure and frustration were actually laying the foundation for the understandings that have created the new level of living I now enjoy."

— Anthony Robbins

#78

"Formal education will make you a living; self—education will make you a fortune."

— Jim Rohn

#79

"You're off to Great Places!

Today is your day!

Your mountain is waiting,

So... get on your way!"

— Dr. Seuss

#80

"Change your thoughts and you change your world."

— Norman Vincent Peale

#81

"One love, one heart, one destiny."

— Bob Marley

#82

"If you have everything under control, you're not moving fast enough."

—Mario Andretti

#83

"Don't judge each day by the harvest you reap but by the seeds that you plant."

— Robert Louis Stevenson

#84

"I do not fear death. I had been dead for billions and billions of years before I was born, and had not suffered the slightest inconvenience from it."

— Mark Twain

#85

"Never let your sense of morals prevent you from doing what is right."

— Isaac Asimov

#86

"Only in the darkness can you see the stars."

— Martin Luther King Jr.

#87

"Do not go where the path may lead, go instead where there is no path and leave a trail."

— Ralph Waldo Emerson

#88

"Why didn't I learn to treat everything like it was the last time. My greatest regret was how much I believed in the future."

— Jonathan Safran Foer

#89

"Your imagination is your preview of life's coming attractions."

—Albert Einstein

#90

"The world is indeed full of peril, and in it there are many dark places; but still there is much that is fair, and though in all lands love is now mingled with grief, it grows perhaps the greater."

— J.R.R. Tolkien

#91

"Turn your wounds into wisdom.

— Oprah Winfrey

#92

"I love to see a young girl go out and grab the world by the lapels. Life's a bitch. You've got to go out and kick ass."

— Maya Angelou

#93

To avoid criticism, do nothing, say nothing, be nothing."

—Elbert Hubbard

#94

"Never let your memories be greater than your dreams."

—Doug Ivester

#95

"War is peace.

Freedom is slavery.

Ignorance is strength."

— George Orwell

#96

"Sometimes our light goes out, but is blown again into instant flame by an encounter with another human being."

— **Albert Schweitzer**

#97

"I don't trust people who don't love themselves and tell me, 'I love you.' ... There is an African saying which is: Be careful when a naked person offers you a shirt."

— **Maya Angelou**

#98

"If you're reading this... Congratulations, you're alive. If that's not something to smile about, then I don't know what is."

— **Chad Sugg**

#99

"If you can't fly then run, if you can't run then walk, if you can't walk then crawl, but whatever you do you have to keep moving forward."

— **Martin Luther King Jr.**

#100

"I am not sure exactly what heaven will be like, but I know that when we die and it comes time for God to judge us, he will not ask, 'How many good things have you done in your life?' rather he will ask,

'How much love did you put into what you did?"

— Mother Teresa

#101

"The secret of health for both mind and body is not to mourn for the past, nor to worry about the future, but to live the present moment wisely and earnestly."

— Gautama Buddha

#102

"The creation of a thousand forests is in one acorn."

—Ralph Waldo Emerson

#103

"To me, Fearless is not the absense of fear. It's not being completely unafraid. To me, Fearless is having fears. Fearless is having doubts. Lots of them. To me, Fearless is living in spite of those things that scare you to death."

— Taylor Swift

#104

"Most of the important things in the world have been accomplished by people who have kept on trying when there seemed to be no help at all."

—Dale Carnegie

#105

"No one has ever become poor by giving."

—Anne Frank

#106

"Don't let the fear of losing be greater than the excitement of winning."

—Robert Kiyosaki

#107

"Every problem is a gift — without problems we would not grow."

— Anthony Robbins

#108

I've learned that people will forget what you said, people will forget what you did, but people will never forget how you made them feel.

—Maya Angelou

#109

I am not a product of my circumstances. I am a product of my decisions.

—Stephen Covey

#110

The most difficult thing is the decision to act, the rest is merely tenacity.

—Amelia Earhart

#111

Whether you think you can or you think you can't, you're right.

—Henry Ford

#112

"Courage is the first of human qualities because it is the quality which guarantees all others."

– Winston Churchill

#113

"Don't be afraid of your fears. They're not there to scare you. They're there to let you know that something is worth it."

— C. JoyBell C.

#114

"Choosing a goal and sticking to it changes everything."

—Scott Reed

#115

"Comparison is the thief of joy."

—Theodore Roosevelt

#116

"Life is a shipwreck, but we must not forget to sing in the lifeboats."

— Voltaire

#117

"We find greatest joy, not in getting, but in expressing what we are. Men do not really live for honors or for pay; their gladness is not the taking and holding, but in doing, the striving, the building, the living. It is a higher joy to teach than to be taught. It is good to get justice, but better to do it; fun to have things but more to make them. The happy man is he who lives the life of love, not for the honors it may bring, but for the life itself."

—R.J. Baughan

#118

"It is not the critic who counts; not the man who points out how the strong man stumbles, or where the doer of deeds could have done them better. The credit belongs to the man who is actually in the arena, whose face is marred by dust and sweat and blood; who strives valiantly; who errs, who comes short again and again, because there is no effort without error and shortcoming; but who does actually strive to do the deeds; who knows great enthusiasms, the great devotions; who spends himself in a worthy cause; who at the best knows in the end the triumph of high achievement, and who at the worst, if he fails, at least fails while daring greatly, so that his place shall never be with those cold and timid souls who neither know victory nor defeat."

— Theodore Roosevelt

#119

"We haven't all had the good fortune to be ladies; we haven't all been generals, or poets, or statesmen; but when the toast works down to the babies, we stand on common ground."

—Mark Twain

#120

Build your own dreams, or someone else will hire you to build theirs.

—Farrah Gray

#121

"Joy goes against the foundations of mathematics: it multiplies when we divide."

—Paulo Coelho

#122

"We are just an advanced breed of monkeys on a minor planet of a very average star. But we can understand the Universe. That makes us something very special."

— Stephen Hawking

#123

"And in the end it is not the years in your life that count, it's the life in your years."

— **Abraham Lincoln**

#124

"Love is not patronizing and charity isn't about pity, it is about love. Charity and love are the same—with charity you give love, so don't just give money but reach out your hand instead."

—**Mother Teresa**

#125

"A ship is safe in harbor, but that's not what ships are for."

— **William G.T. Shedd**

#126

"I was smiling yesterday,I am smiling today and I will smile tomorrow.Simply because life is too short to cry for anything."

— **Santosh Kalwar**

#127

"If you are irritated by every rub, how will your mirror be polished?"

— **Rumi**

#128

"Joy is what happens to us when we allow ourselves to recognize how good things really are."

—Marianne Williamson

#129

Remember that not getting what you want is sometimes a wonderful stroke of luck.

—Dalai Lama

#130

"Life begins at the end of your comfort zone."

—Neale Donald Walsch

#131

"Joy is the holy fire that keeps our purpose warm and our intelligence aglow."

—Helen Keller

#132

"Maybe everyone can live beyond what they're capable of."

— Markus Zusak

#133

"Nothing great was ever achieved without enthusiasm."

— Ralph Waldo Emerson

#134

"Change will not come if we wait for some other person, or if we wait for some other time. We are the ones we've been waiting for. We are the change that we seek."

— Barack Obama

#135

"Trees that are slow to grow bear the best fruit."

— Molière

#136

"I'd rather be hated for who I am, than loved for who I am not."

— Kurt Cobain

#137

"It's easy to find reasons for division between people. Finding common ground is harder, but a step towards happiness."

—Unknown

#138

"My concern is not whether God is on our side; my greatest concern is to be on God's side, for God is always right."

— Abraham Lincoln

#139

Think like a queen. A queen is not afraid to fail. Failure is another steppingstone to greatness.

— Oprah Winfrey

#140

"Reputation is what other people know about you. Honor is what you know about yourself."

— Lois McMaster Bujold

#141

"What's the good of living if you don't try a few things?"

— Charles M. Schulz

#142

"I have come to accept the feeling of not knowing where I am going. And I have trained myself to love it. Because it is only when we are suspended in mid—air with no landing in sight, that we force our wings to unravel and alas begin our flight. And as we fly, we still may not know where we are going to. But the miracle is in the unfolding of the wings. You may not know where you're going, but you know that so long as you spread your wings, the winds will carry you."

— C. JoyBell C.

#143

"Kindness is a language which the deaf can hear and the blind can see."

— Mark Twain

#144

"Anyone can hide. Facing up to things, working through them, that's what makes you strong."

— Sarah Dessen

#145

"It's not the size of the dog in the fight, it's the size of the fight in the dog."

— Mark Twain

#146

I have learned over the years that when one's mind is made up, this diminishes fear.

—Rosa Parks

#147

"Great heroes need great sorrows and burdens, or half their greatness goes unnoticed. It is all part of the fairy tale."

— Peter S. Beagle

#148

"When I was about eight, I decided that the most wonderful thing, next to a human being, was a book."

— Margaret Walker

#149

"If you think you are too small to make a difference, try sleeping with a mosquito."

— Dalai Lama

#150

"Nothing in the world is ever completely wrong. Even a stopped clock is right twice a day."

— Paulo Coelho

#151

"What do we live for, if it is not to make life less difficult for each other?"

— George Eliot

#152

"If we did all the things we are capable of, we would literally astound ourselves."

— Thomas A. Edison

#153

"If you don't go after what you want, you'll never have it. If you don't ask, the answer is always no. If you don't step forward, you're always in the same place."

— **Nora Roberts**

#154

"A concept is a brick. It can be used to build a courthouse of reason. Or it can be thrown through the window."

— **Gilles Deleuze**

#155

"Whatever you do, you need courage. Whatever course you decide upon, there is always someone to tell you that you are wrong. There are always difficulties arising that tempt you to believe your critics are right. To map out a course of action and follow it to an end requires some of the same courage that a soldier needs. Peace has its victories, but it takes brave men and women to win them."

— **Ralph Waldo Emerson**

#156

"We can't help everyone, but everyone can help someone."

— **Ronald Reagan**

#157

I would rather die of passion than of boredom.

—Vincent van Gogh

#158

"Vitality shows in not only the ability to persist but the ability to start over."

— F. Scott Fitzgerald

#159

"Walk with the dreamers, the believers, the courageous, the cheerful, the planners, the doers, the successful people with their heads in the clouds and their feet on the ground. Let their spirit ignite a fire within you to leave this world better than when you found it."

—Wilferd A. Peterson

#160

"It's not what you look at that matters, it's what you see."

— Henry David Thoreau

#161

"No matter how your heart is grieving, if you keep on believing, the dreams that you wish will come true."

— Walt Disney Company

#162

"The real heroes anyway aren't the people doing things; the real heroes are the people NOTICING things, paying attention."

— John Green

#163

"The desire to reach for the stars is ambitious. The desire to reach hearts is wise."

— Maya Angelou

#164

What God intended for you goes far beyond anything you can imagine.

— Oprah Winfrey

#165

"If you make a mistake and do not correct it, this is called a mistake."

— Confucius

#166

"Learn to love without condition. Talk without bad intention. Give without any reason. And most of all, care for people without any expectation."

—Unknown

#167

"Do the things you used to talk about doing but never did. Know when to let go and when to hold on tight. Stop rushing. Don't be intimidated to say it like it is. Stop apologizing all the time. Learn to say no, so your yes has some oomph. Spend time with the friends who lift you up, and cut loose the ones who bring you down. Stop giving your power away. Be more concerned with being interested than being interesting. Be old enough to appreciate your freedom, and young enough to enjoy it. Finally, know who you are."

—Kristin Armstrong

#168

"It had long since come to my attention that people of accomplishment rarely sat back and let things happen to them. They went out and happened to things."

—Leonardo da Vinci

#169

The question isn't who is going to let me; it's who is going to stop me.

—Ayn Rand

#170

"If you shift your focus from yourself to others, extend your concern to others, and cultivate the thought of caring for the well being of others, then this will have the immediate effect of opening up your life and helping you to reach out."

—Dalai Lama

#171

"We can learn to see each other and see ourselves in each other and recognize that human beings are more alike than we are unalike."

—Maya Angelou

#172

"How far you go in life depends on your being tender with the young, compassionate with the aged, sympathetic with the striving and tolerant of the weak and strong. —Because someday in your life you will have been all of these."

—George Washington Carver

#173

The biggest adventure you can take is to live the life of your dreams.

— Oprah Winfrey

#174

A truly rich man is one whose children run into his arms when his hands are empty.

—Unknown

#175

"While we do our good works let us not forget that the real solution lies in a world in which charity will have become unnecessary."

—Chinua Achebe

#176

"You must take personal responsibility. You cannot change the circumstances, the seasons, or the wind, but you can change yourself. That is something you have charge of."

—Jim Rohn

#177

"Health is the greatest gift, contentment the greatest wealth, faithfulness the best relationship."

— Buddha

#178

"The best day of your life is the one on which you decide your life is your own. No apologies or excuses. No one to lean on, rely on, or blame. The gift is yours — it is an amazing journey — and you alone are responsible for the quality of it. This is the day your life really begins."

—Bob Moawad

#179

"When we give cheerfully and accept gratefully, everyone is blessed."

—Maya Angelou

#180

The only way to do great work is to love what you do.

—Steve Jobs

#181

"Find joy in everything you choose to do. Every job, relationship, home... it's your responsibility to love it, or change it."

—Chuck Palahniuk

#182

"When one tugs at a single thing in nature, he finds it attached to the rest of the world."

—John Muir

#183

If you hear a voice within you say "you cannot paint," then by all means paint and that voice will be silenced.

—Vincent Van Gogh

#184

"Your opponent, in the end, is never really the player on the other side of the net, or the swimmer in the next lane, or the team on the other side of the field, or even the bar you must high—jump. Your opponent is yourself, your negative internal voices, —your level of determination."

—Grace Lichtenstein

#185

"To practice five things under all circumstances constitutes perfect virtue; these five are gravity, generosity of soul, sincerity, earnestness, and kindness."

—Confucius

#186

"Motivation is what gets you started. Habit is what keeps you going. "

—Jim Ryun

#187

Surround yourself with only people who are going to lift you higher.

— Oprah Winfrey

#188

"The most beautiful people we have known are those who have known defeat, known suffering, known struggle, known loss, and have found their way out of the depths. These persons have an appreciation, a sensitivity, and an understanding of life that fills them with compassion, gentleness, and a deep loving concern. Beautiful people do not just happen."

— Elisabeth Kübler—Ross

#189

"We don't beat the Grim Reaper by living longer, we beat the Reaper by living well and living fully, for the Reaper will come for all of us. The question is what do we do between the time we are born and the time he shows up."

— Randy Pausch

#190

"Service is a smile. It is an acknowledging wave, a reaching handshake, a friendly wink, and a warm hug. It's these simple acts that matter most, because the greatest service to a human soul has always been the kindness of recognition."

— Richelle E. Goodrich

#191

"Do you want to know who you are? Don't ask. Act! Action will delineate and define you."

— Thomas Jefferson

#192

If you want to lift yourself up, lift up someone else.

—Booker T. Washington

#193

"Take care of your body. It's the only place you have to live."

—Jim Rohn

#194

"The road to Easy Street goes through the sewer."

—John Madden

#195

I still have my feet on the ground, I just wear better shoes.

— Oprah Winfrey

#196

"Health is the greatest of all possessions; a pale cobbler is better than a sick king."

—Jonathan Swift

#197

"Love is the absence of judgment."

— Dalai Lama

#198

"I dream my painting and I paint my dream."

— Vincent van Gogh

#199

"We cannot seek achievement for ourselves and forget about progress and prosperity for our community...Our ambitions must be broad enough to include the aspirations and needs of others, for their sakes and for our own."

—Cesar Chavez

#200

"The wise do not buy into other people's perceptions of who they are and what they are capable of. Instead, they bypass a person's public persona and see who they are in their highest expression. When you see actions taken with integrity, instead of words only, you will then know a soul's worth."

—Shannon L. Alder

#201

"A generous heart, kind speech, and a life of service and compassion are the things which renew humanity."

—Buddha

#202

"I know you've heard it a thousand times before, but it's true... hard work pays off. If you want to be good, you have to practice, practice, practice. If you don't love something, then don't do it."

—Ray Bradbury

#203

"Victory is remembered for at most two decades; an act of good sportsmanship is remembered for a lifetime."

—Simon Nguyen

#204

"That thing that you do, after your day job, in your free time, too early in the morning, too late at night. That thing you read about, write about, think about, in fact fantasize about. That thing you do when you're all alone and there's no one to impress, nothing to prove, no money to be made, simply a passion to pursue. That's it. That's your thing. That's your heart, your guide. That's the thing you must, must do."

—Jes Allen

#205

"You yourself, as much as anybody in the entire universe, deserve your love and affection"

— Gautama Buddha

#206

"The best and most beautiful things in the world cannot be seen or even touched — they must be felt with the heart."

—Helen Keller

#207

"Accept responsibility for your life. Know that it is you who will get you where you want to go, no one else."

—Les Brown

#208

"Courage is what it takes to stand up and speak; courage is also what it takes to sit down and listen."

—Winston Churchill

#209

"Confront the dark parts of yourself, and work to banish them with illumination and forgiveness. Your willingness to wrestle with your demons will cause your angels to sing."

—August Wilson

#210

"There are years that ask questions and years that answer."

— Zora Neale Hurston

#211

"For to be free is not merely to cast off one's chains, but to live in a way that respects and enhances the freedom of others."

—Nelson Mandela

#212

"An ounce of practice is generally worth more than a ton of theory."

—Ernst F. Schumacher

#213

"Make the most of yourself....for that is all there is of you."

— Ralph Waldo Emerson

#214

"It is easy in the world to live after the world's opinion; it is easy in solitude to live after our own; but the great man is he who in the midst of the crowd keeps with perfect sweetness the independence of solitude."

— Ralph Waldo Emerson

#215

"Every strike brings me closer to the next home run."

—Babe Ruth

#216

"If we have no peace, it is because we have forgotten that we belong to each other."

— Mother Teresa

#217

"To love and win is the best thing. To love and lose, the next best."

— William Makepeace Thackeray

#218

"Inspiration and genius—one and the same."

—Victor Hugo

#219

"Freedom is not the absence of commitments, but the ability to choose — and commit myself to — what is best for me."

—Paulo Coelho

#220

"Be of good cheer. Do not think of today's failures, but of the success that may come tomorrow. You have set yourselves a difficult task, but you will succeed if you persevere; and you will find a joy in overcoming obstacles. Remember, no effort that we make to attain something beautiful is ever lost."

—Helen Keller

#221

"The best thing to hold onto in life is each other."

— Audrey Hepburn

#222

"If it doesn't challenge you, it doesn't change you."

—Fred DeVito

#223

"Nothing is worth more than this day.

You cannot relive yesterday.

Tomorrow is still beyond our reach."

—Johann Wolfgang Von Goethe

#224

"It takes two flints to make a fire."

—Louisa May Alcott

#225

"Believe you can and you're halfway there."

—Theodore Roosevelt

#226

"If you want to go fast, go alone. If you want to go far, go together."

—African Proverb

#227

Limitations live only in our minds. But if we use our imaginations, our possibilities become limitless.

—Jamie Paolinetti

#228

"Sometimes its not the strength but gentleness that cracks the hardest shells."

—Richard Paul Evans

#229

"Without commitment, you cannot have depth in anything, whether it's a relationship, a business or a hobby."

—Neil Strauss

#230

"I was always looking outside myself for strength and confidence, but it comes from within. It is there all of the time."

—Anna Freud

#231

"Wilderness is not a luxury, but a necessity of the human spirit."

—Edward Abbey

#232

"Talent wins games, but teamwork wins championships."

—Michael Jordan

#233

Lots of people want to ride with you in the limo, but what you want is someone who will take the bus with you when the limo breaks down.

— Oprah Winfrey

#234

"Excellence is the result of caring more than others think is wise, risking more than others think is safe, dreaming more than others think is practical, and expecting more than others think is possible."

—Ronnie Oldham

#235

How wonderful it is that nobody need wait a single moment before starting to improve the world.

—Anne Frank

#236

"I always wondered why somebody didn't do something about that; then I realized that I am somebody."

—Unknown

#237

Believe you can and you're halfway there.

—Theodore Roosevelt

#238

"Unity is strength... when there is teamwork and collaboration, wonderful things can be achieved."

—Mattie Stepanek

#239

"I avoid looking forward or backward, and try to keep looking upward."

—Charlotte Brontë

#240

"Earth provides enough to satisfy every man's needs, but not every man's greed."

— Mahatma Gandhi

#241

"Every artist was first an amateur."

—Ralph Waldo Emerson

#242

The only person you are destined to become is the person you decide to be.

—Ralph Waldo Emerson

#243

"In any project the important factor is your belief. Without belief, there can be no successful outcome."

—William James

#244

"The earth has music for those who listen."

—George Santayana

#245

To handle yourself, use your head; to handle others, use your heart.

—Eleanor Roosevelt

#246

Be thankful for what you have; you'll end up having more. If you concentrate on what you don't have, you will never, ever have enough.

— Oprah Winfrey

#247

"Have courage for the great sorrows of life and patience for the small ones; and when you have laboriously accomplished your daily task, go to sleep in peace. God is awake."

— Victor Hugo

#248

"Life has no smooth road for any of us; and in the bracing atmosphere of a high aim the very roughness stimulates the climber to steadier steps, till the legend, over steep ways to the stars, fulfills itself."

—W. C. Doane

#249

We can't help everyone, but everyone can help someone.

—Ronald Reagan

#250

"Imagination is everything. It is the preview of life's coming attractions."

— Albert Einstein

#251

"The more difficulties one has to encounter, within and without, the more significant and the higher in inspiration his life will be."

—Horace Bushnell

#252

"Don't wait. The time will never be just right."

—Napoleon Hill

#253

"The most beautiful things in the world cannot be seen or touched, they are felt with the heart."

— Antoine de Saint-Exupéry

#254

"Don't count the days, make the days count."

—Muhammad Ali

#255

Too many of us are not living our dreams because we are living our fears.

—Les Brown

#256

"We don't make mistakes, just happy little accidents."

— Bob Ross

#257

We can easily forgive a child who is afraid of the dark; the real tragedy of life is when men are afraid of the light.

—Plato

#258

"Courage doesn't always roar. Sometimes courage is the little voice at the end of the day that says I'll try again tomorrow."

—Mary Anne Radmacher

#259

Nothing will work unless you do.

—Maya Angelou

#260

"Change is not something that we should fear. Rather, it is something that we should welcome. For without change, nothing in this world would ever grow or blossom, and no one in this world would ever move forward to become the person they're meant to be."

—B.K.S. Iyengar

#261

"I must be willing to give up what I am in order to become what I will be."

— Albert Einstein

#262

"The difference between ordinary and extraordinary is that little extra."

—Jimmy Johnson

#263

"If I had to select one quality, one personal characteristic that I regard as being most highly correlated with success, whatever the field, I would pick the trait of persistence. Determination. The will to endure to the end, to get knocked down seventy times and get up off the floor saying, "Here comes number seventy—one!""

—Richard DeVos

#264

"Dream big and dare to fail."

—Norman Vaughan

#265

"If you can't you must, and if you must you can."

— Anthony Robbins

#266

"To give pleasure to a single heart by a single act is better than a thousand heads bowing in prayer."

— Mahatma Gandhi

#267

"Happy are those who dream dreams and are ready to pay the price to make them come true."

—Leon J. Suenes

#268

Everything you've ever wanted is on the other side of fear.

—George Addair

#269

"Risks must be taken because the greatest hazard in life is to risk nothing."

— Leo Buscaglia

#270

"Success is going from failure to failure without losing your enthusiasm."

—Winston Churchill

#271

"If you would create something,

you must be something."

—Johann Wolfgang von Goethe

#272

Perfection is not attainable, but if we chase perfection we can catch excellence.

—Vince Lombardi

#273

I can't change the direction of the wind, but I can adjust my sails to always reach my destination.

—Jimmy Dean

#274

"Believe and act as if it were impossible to fail."

—Charles Kettering

#275

"He that can have patience can have what he will."

— Benjamin Franklin

#276

"Not being heard is no reason for silence."

— Victor Hugo

#277

"Our wounds are often the openings into the best and most beautiful part of us."

— David Richo

#278

"Tough times never last, but tough people do."

—Dr. Robert Schuller

#279

"When all is said and done, more is said than done."

— Lou Holtz

#280

"The greatest disease in the West today is not TB or leprosy; it is being unwanted, unloved, and uncared for. We can cure physical diseases with medicine, but the only cure for loneliness, despair, and hopelessness is love. There are many in the world who are dying for a piece of bread but there are many more dying for a little love. The poverty in the West is a different kind of poverty —— it is not only a poverty of loneliness but also of spirituality. There's a hunger for love, as there is a hunger for God."

— Mother Teresa

#281

Make each day your masterpiece."

— John Wooden

#282

"You'll never get ahead of anyone as long as you try to get even with him."

— Lou Holtz

#283

"The best dreams happen when you're awake."

—Cherie Gilderbloom

#284

"You'll never find a rainbow if you're looking down"

— **Charles Chaplin**

#285

"Always remember, your focus determines your reality."

— **George Lucas**

#286

There is only one success: to be able to spend your life in your own way."

—**Christopher Morley**

#287

"Genius is one percent inspiration, ninety—nine percent perspiration."

— **Thomas A. Edison**

#288

"Experience is the child of thought, and thought is the child of action."

—**Benjamin Disraeli**

#289

"When we give cheerfully and accept gratefully, everyone is blessed."

— Maya Angelou

#290

"Those who look for the bad in people will surely find it."

— Abraham Lincoln

#291

"We can do anything we want to do if we stick to it long enough."

—Helen Keller

#292

"The journey of a thousand miles begins with one step."

— Lao Tzu

#293

"First say to yourself what you would be;

and then do what you have to do."

—Epictetus

#294

"The best way out is always through."

—Robert Frost

#295

The most common way people give up their power is by thinking they don't have any.

—Alice Walker

#296

"Too often we underestimate the power of a touch, a smile, a kind word, a listening ear, an honest compliment, or the smallest act of caring, all of which have the potential to turn a life around."

— Leo Buscaglia

#297

It is during our darkest moments that we must focus to see the light.

—Aristotle Onassis

#298

"Courage isn't having the strength to go on — it is going on when you don't have strength."

— Napoléon Bonaparte

#299

"Take it easy, but take it."

— Woody Guthrie

#300

"Oh the places you'll go! There is fun to be done! There are points to be scored. There are games to be won. And the magical things you can do with that ball will make you the winning—est winner of all."

— Dr. Seuss

#301

"If we have no peace, it is because we have forgotten that we belong to each other."

— Mother Teresa

#302

Life is 10% what happens to me and 90% of how I react to it.

—Charles Swindoll

#303

"We either make ourselves miserable, or we make ourselves strong. The amount of work is the same."

— Carlos Castaneda

#304

"I have not the shadow of a doubt that any man or woman can achieve what I have, if he or she will make the same effort, and have the same hope and faith."

—Mahatma Gandhi

#305

"Once you choose hope, anything's possible."

—Christopher Reeve

#306

"Keep your face always toward the sunshine — and shadows will fall behind you."

— Walt Whitman

#307

"Do we not all agree to call rapid thought and noble impulse by the name of inspiration?"

—George Eliot

#308

"Believe you can and you're halfway there."

— Theodore Roosevelt

#309

Do the one thing you think you cannot do. Fail at it. Try again. Do better the second time. The only people who never tumble are those who never mount the high wire. This is your moment. Own it.

— Oprah Winfrey

#310

"The price of greatness is responsibility."

— Winston S. Churchill

#311

"Without fear there cannot be courage."

— Christopher Paolini

#312

"What difference do it make if the thing you scared of is real or not?"

— Toni Morrison

#313

"No great man ever complains of want of opportunities."

—Ralph Waldo Emerson

#314

"You cannot expect victory and plan for defeat."

— Joel Osteen

#315

"Men do less than they ought,

unless they do all they can."

—Thomas Carlyle

#316

"When I let go of what I am, I become what I might be."

— Lao Tzu

#317

"We all pay for life with death, so everything in between should be free."

— Bill Hicks

#318

Make each day your masterpiece."

—John Wooden

#319

"The reason birds can fly and we can't is simply because they have perfect faith, for to have faith is to have wings."

— J.M. Barrie

#320

"The power of imagination makes us infinite."

—John Muir

#321

"Everybody is special. Everybody. Everybody is a hero, a lover, a fool, a villain. Everybody. Everybody has their story to tell."

— Alan Moore

#322

I alone cannot change the world, but I can cast a stone across the water to create many ripples.

—Mother Teresa

#323

"Don't wait for extraordinary opportunities. Seize common occasions and make them great."

—Orison Swett Marden

#324

What's money? A man is a success if he gets up in the morning and goes to bed at night and in between does what he wants to do.

—Bob Dylan

#325

"Death is no more than passing from one room into another. But there's a difference for me, you know. Because in that other room I shall be able to see."

— Helen Keller

#326

"The best things in life make you sweaty."

— Edgar Allan Poe

#327

"There's so much to be grateful for, words are poor things."

— Marilynne Robinson

#328

"For myself I am an optimist — it does not seem to be much use to be anything else."

— Winston S. Churchill

#329

"The biggest adventure you can ever take is to live the life of your dreams."

— Oprah Winfrey

#330

"Every moment is a fresh beginning."

—T.S. Eliot

#331

What we achieve inwardly will change outer reality.

—Plutarch

#332

"I live my life in widening circles that reach out across the world."

— **Rainer Maria Rilke**

#333

"Everything can be taken from a man but one thing: the last of the human freedoms—to choose one's attitude in any given set of circumstances, to choose one's own way."

— **Viktor E. Frankl**

#334

"I like nonsense, it wakes up the brain cells. Fantasy is a necessary ingredient in living, It's a way of looking at life through the wrong end of a telescope. Which is what I do, And that enables you to laugh at life's realities."

— **Dr. Seuss**

#335

"We are products of our past, but we don't have to be prisoners of it."

— **Rick Warren**

#336

"Around here, however, we don't look backwards for very long. We keep moving forward, opening up new doors and doing new things, because we're curious...and curiosity keeps leading us down new paths."

— Walt Disney Company

#337

If you're offered a seat on a rocket ship, don't ask what seat! Just get on.

—Sheryl Sandberg

#338

"Just be yourself, there is no one better."

— Taylor Swift

#339

"The higher we soar the smaller we appear to those who cannot fly."

— Friedrich Nietzsche

#340

"Excellence is never an accident. It is always the result of high intention, sincere effort, and intelligent execution; it represents the wise choice of many alternatives — choice, not chance, determines your destiny."

— Aristotle

#341

"Change the way you look at things and the things you look at change."

— Wayne W. Dyer

#342

"The journey of a thousand miles begins with one step."

—Lao Tzu

#343

"God allows us to experience the low points of life in order to teach us lessons that we could learn in no other way."

— C.S. Lewis

#344

"I shall look at you out of the corner of my eye, and you will say nothing. Words are the source of misunderstandings."

— Antoine de Saint-Exupéry

#345

"For me, I am driven by two main philosophies: know more today about the world than I knew yesterday and lessen the suffering of others. You'd be surprised how far that gets you."

— Neil deGrasse Tyson

#346

"We delight in the beauty of the butterfly, but rarely admit the changes it has gone through to achieve that beauty."

— Maya Angelou

#347

"The flower that blooms in adversity is the rarest and most beautiful of all."

— Walt Disney Company

#348

Certain things catch your eye, but pursue only those that capture the heart.

—Ancient Indian Proverb

#349

I have been impressed with the urgency of doing. Knowing is not enough; we must apply. Being willing is not enough; we must do.

—Leonardo da Vinci

#350

Everything has beauty, but not everyone can see.

—Confucius

#351

"No one really knows why they are alive until they know what they'd die for."

— Martin Luther King Jr.

#352

"You must not only aim right, but draw the bow with all your might."

—Henry David Thoreau

#353

"The unexamined life is not worth living."

— Socrates

#354

"A man with outward courage dares to die; a man with inner courage dares to live."

— Lao Tzu

#355

"Courage is the most important of all the virtues because without courage, you can't practice any other virtue consistently."

— Maya Angelou

#356

A person who never made a mistake never tried anything new.

—Albert Einstein

#356

"The greatest thing in the world is to know how to belong to oneself."

— Michel de Montaigne

#357

"No! Try not. Do, or do not. There is no try."

— George Lucas

#358

"Wherever you go, go with all your heart."

— Confucius

#359

"Don't ever take a fence down until you know why it was put up."

— Robert Frost

#360

"Let us rise up and be thankful, for if we didn't learn a lot at least we learned a little, and if we didn't learn a little, at least we didn't get sick, and if we got sick, at least we didn't die; so, let us all be thankful."

— Gautama Buddha

#361

"Life was meant to be lived, and curiosity must be kept alive. One must never, for whatever reason, turn his back on life."

— Eleanor Roosevelt

#362

"Go confidently in the direction of your dreams. Live the life you've imagined."

— Henry David Thoreau

#363

"Whether you live to be 50 or 100 makes no difference, if you made no difference in the world."

— Jarod Kintz

#364

"Be more concerned with your character than your reputation, because your character is what you really are, while your reputation is merely what others think you are."

— John Wooden

#365

"Dream as if you will live forever; Live as if you will die today."

— James Dean

CONCLUSION

I am really happy you went through all 365 quotes and at the same time I hope you got inspired by these quotes and now look at the world though different lenses. I hope you will use these quotes into your advantage, make your life better, and make this world a better place.

Thank you for reading this book.

Made in United States
Orlando, FL
04 March 2023

30676418R00046